The Ultimate Guide to Surviving an Economic Collapse

The Ultimate Guide to Surviving an Economic Collapse

Petchinsky

1

The Ultimate Guide to Surviving an Economic Collapse

By: Matthew Petchinsky

Introduction: How to Prepare and Thrive in Times of Financial Crisis

The modern world operates on the foundation of economic stability—markets rise and fall, businesses open and close, and governments print and control currency to manage the financial ecosystem. However, history has shown us time and time again that economies are anything but predictable. From the Great Depression of the 1930s to the global financial crisis of 2008, and the more recent economic turmoil caused by pandemics, supply chain disruptions, inflation, and geopolitical conflicts, one thing remains constant: economic collapses are not a matter of *if* but *when.*

Yet, in the face of such uncertainty, the difference between devastation and security comes down to one thing—*preparedness*. The individuals, families, and businesses that survive and even thrive during economic crises are not the ones who panic when disaster strikes; they are the ones who anticipated the storm, built their financial lifeboats, and took action long before the crisis hit.

This book, *The Ultimate Guide to Surviving an Economic Collapse*, is your roadmap to financial resilience. Whether you're facing skyrocketing inflation, job loss, supply shortages, or the collapse of financial institutions, this guide will equip you with the knowledge, skills, and strategies necessary to withstand and even prosper during times of economic turmoil.

Understanding Economic Collapse: Why It Happens and What It Means for You

An economic collapse occurs when financial systems and markets experience a rapid and severe decline, often leading to mass unemployment, hyperinflation or deflation, business closures, banking failures, and a breakdown of essential services. The consequences of such an event ripple through every aspect of daily life—food prices soar, savings lose value, governments impose strict financial controls, and access to credit becomes nearly impossible.

While each economic downturn has unique causes, the underlying triggers typically include:

- **Unsustainable Debt Levels** – When governments, corporations, and individuals take on excessive debt, it creates an unstable financial structure that can collapse under economic pressure.
- **Inflation and Currency Devaluation** – When money loses purchasing power due to excessive printing or loss of trust in the currency, everyday essentials become unaffordable.
- **Stock Market Crashes** – A sudden decline in stock prices can erase wealth overnight, leading to panic and further economic contraction.
- **Banking Failures and Credit Freezes** – When banks collapse, access to funds becomes restricted, making it difficult to conduct business or even withdraw personal savings.
- **Supply Chain Disruptions** – Pandemics, war, and natural disasters can halt production and distribution, leading to shortages of food, medicine, and critical goods.
- **Government Policies and Overreach** – Economic mismanagement, excessive taxation, and poor fiscal policies can accelerate financial instability.

While these crises are often outside of individual control, how you prepare for them is *completely within your control.*

Mindset Shift: From Panic to Preparedness

The first step in surviving an economic collapse isn't about money—it's about *mindset.* Fear and panic lead to impulsive decisions, while preparation and knowledge lead to security. Developing a *survival mindset* means:

1. **Accepting Harsh Realities Early** – The sooner you recognize economic vulnerabilities, the more time you have to prepare.
2. **Becoming Self-Reliant** – Reduce dependence on fragile financial systems and government aid by taking control of your finances, food supply, and resources.
3. **Building Multiple Income Streams** – If one source of income disappears, you have others to fall back on.
4. **Focusing on Long-Term Sustainability** – Rather than reacting to short-term chaos, build a foundation that ensures long-term survival and success.
5. **Being Adaptable** – Economic collapses create unpredictable environments. The more adaptable you are, the better you'll thrive.

The Three Pillars of Economic Survival: Finance, Resources, and Community

In times of financial crisis, your ability to weather the storm depends on three key pillars:

1. **Financial Preparedness** – A strong financial foundation is essential. This includes:
    - Reducing and eliminating debt to avoid financial traps.
    - Creating multiple income streams to diversify risk.
    - Holding emergency savings in a form that retains value, such as precious metals or stable currencies.
    - Understanding barter and alternative trade systems for when traditional money becomes unreliable.
2. **Resource Management** – Having access to essential resources ensures survival when supply chains break down:
    - **Food Security** – Stockpile non-perishable food, learn to grow your own, and develop food preservation skills.
    - **Water Supply** – Store potable water and learn purification methods.
    - **Energy Independence** – Solar power, generators, and alternative heating sources can keep your household running when utilities fail.
    - **Security and Protection** – Economic crises often lead to increased crime. Being prepared with self-defense training and home security is crucial.
3. **Community and Networking** – No one thrives in isolation. Economic collapse affects entire populations, making strong communities invaluable:
    - **Trade and Bartering** – Establish local networks where people exchange goods and services without relying on money.

- **Mutual Aid** – Working together with family, friends, and neighbors increases collective survival chances.
- **Local Skill-Sharing** – Learn and teach valuable survival skills like food production, first aid, and repair work.

Thriving Beyond Survival: Turning Crisis into Opportunity

While surviving an economic collapse is the primary goal, true resilience means learning how to *thrive* despite financial uncertainty. Many of the wealthiest and most successful individuals in history built their fortunes *during* economic downturns by recognizing opportunities in crisis. You can do the same by:

- **Investing Wisely** – In every crisis, some assets lose value while others gain. Understanding which industries and commodities remain strong can help you make smart investments.
- **Developing In-Demand Skills** – Learning high-value skills such as self-sufficiency, repair work, and alternative medicine can create income opportunities even in economic hardship.
- **Building an Online Presence** – Digital entrepreneurship, content creation, and e-commerce provide income streams independent of local economic collapse.
- **Creating a Legacy of Preparedness** – Teaching your family and community how to prepare ensures generational resilience against future crises.

Final Thoughts: The Future Belongs to the Prepared

Economic collapses are inevitable, but financial ruin is *not*. Those who prepare wisely, develop self-reliance, and build strong financial and resource-based foundations will not only survive but *thrive* in times of crisis.

This book will take you through every aspect of economic survival—how to protect your wealth, secure essential resources, create sustainable income, and navigate societal changes with confidence. By the time you finish reading, you will be fully equipped to face any financial disaster with a clear plan, a resilient mindset, and the skills needed to emerge stronger than ever.

Now, let's begin your journey to financial survival and success.

Chapter 1: Recognizing the Warning Signs of Economic Collapse

Economic collapses rarely happen overnight. While a sudden financial crash may seem abrupt to the untrained eye, there are always warning signs that precede economic downturns. Recognizing these early indicators can mean the difference between proactive preparation and catastrophic loss. In this chapter, we will explore the key signs of an impending economic collapse, why they matter, and how to interpret them to take timely action.

The Nature of Economic Collapse: Slow Burn or Sudden Crash?

Before delving into the specific warning signs, it's essential to understand how economic collapses typically unfold. There are generally two types of collapses:

1. **Gradual Economic Decline (Slow Burn)** – This occurs over months or even years, with worsening conditions such as rising unemployment, higher inflation, increasing national debt, and growing economic uncertainty. These conditions weaken financial stability until a final breaking point is reached.
2. **Sudden Economic Shock (Rapid Crash)** – These occur when an unexpected event—such as a stock market crash, hyperinflation, war, or a banking crisis—causes an immediate financial breakdown. This type of collapse often leads to bank runs, rapid currency devaluation, and government interventions.

Regardless of the type of collapse, the warning signs are often visible if you know where to look.

Key Warning Signs of an Impending Economic Collapse

1. Increasing National Debt and Deficit Spending

One of the strongest indicators of a looming economic collapse is excessive national debt. When a government continually spends beyond its means without balancing its budget, it creates a financial time bomb.

- A nation with unsustainable debt will eventually be forced to print more money or raise taxes to cover its expenses.
- Printing more money leads to **inflation** (devaluation of currency), while excessive taxation slows economic growth and business activity.
- Countries with high debt-to-GDP ratios (exceeding 100%) are at a higher risk of financial instability.

◈ *What You Can Do:* Monitor government spending and debt levels. If you see increasing debt and little effort to control it, prepare by diversifying assets and securing wealth outside of fiat currency.

2. High Inflation and Hyperinflation

Inflation refers to the rise in the cost of goods and services over time. A controlled level of inflation is normal in a growing economy, but when inflation becomes excessive, it signals deep financial instability.

- **Moderate Inflation (2-5%)** – Often considered manageable, but signals potential future instability.
- **High Inflation (6-15%)** – The cost of living rises rapidly, reducing purchasing power.
- **Hyperinflation (50%+ per month)** – A total economic disaster where currency becomes worthless (e.g., Zimbabwe, Venezuela, Weimar Germany).

Signs that inflation is getting out of control:
◈ Rapid increases in food, gas, and housing prices.
◈ Wages not keeping up with the cost of living.
◈ Shortages of basic necessities as people hoard supplies.

◈ *What You Can Do:* Invest in inflation-resistant assets such as precious metals, real estate, or commodities. Stockpile essential goods before prices skyrocket.

3. Rising Unemployment and Job Losses

A declining economy often results in mass layoffs and business closures. Signs of increasing unemployment include:

- Companies downsizing or freezing hiring.
- Mass layoffs in major industries such as manufacturing, retail, or tech.
- A rise in government unemployment claims.
- More people taking on multiple jobs just to survive.

◈ *What You Can Do:* Strengthen your financial position by developing multiple income streams. Start a side business, learn valuable trades, or invest in recession-proof skills.

4. Bank Instability and Credit Freezes

Banks are the backbone of the financial system. If they begin to struggle, it is a **major red flag** for an impending collapse. Warning signs include:

- **Bank Runs** – When too many people withdraw money at once, fearing a bank collapse.
- **Withdrawal Limits** – Governments or banks restricting access to savings.
- **Bank Failures** – Major financial institutions defaulting on debts or needing bailouts.
- **Tighter Credit Conditions** – Loans and mortgages becoming harder to obtain.

◈ *What You Can Do:* Keep cash reserves on hand, hold some assets outside the banking system (precious metals, cryptocurrencies), and avoid keeping all your wealth in a single institution.

5. Stock Market Crashes and Volatility

While stock markets naturally fluctuate, extreme instability is often a **precursor to economic collapse**. Warning signs in the markets include:

- Major indexes (Dow Jones, S&P 500, Nasdaq) dropping by double digits within weeks or days.
- Massive sell-offs by institutional investors.
- Frequent emergency interventions by governments or central banks.

◈ *What You Can Do:* If you invest, consider shifting to defensive assets such as gold, silver, or stable dividend-paying stocks.

6. Decline in Global Trade and Supply Chain Disruptions

A healthy economy depends on smooth global trade. When supply chains break down, it can lead to product shortages and rising costs. Warning signs include:

- Increased delays in goods delivery.
- High transportation and shipping costs.
- Businesses struggling to source raw materials.
- Geopolitical tensions disrupting international trade.

◈ *What You Can Do:* Stock up on essential goods, learn self-sufficiency skills, and build local supply networks.

7. Social and Political Instability

Financial crises often trigger unrest, leading to protests, riots, and government overreach. Warning signs include:

- Rising crime rates due to economic hardship.
- Widespread protests over cost of living.
- Governments enacting emergency economic measures such as currency controls or wealth seizures.
- Censorship or restricted access to financial resources.

◈ *What You Can Do:* Strengthen personal security, build a reliable community, and diversify your assets globally if possible.

How to Use These Warning Signs to Your Advantage

Recognizing these signs early allows you to **prepare before disaster strikes**. Here's how:

◈ **Monitor financial news and economic reports** – Stay informed on inflation rates, unemployment figures, and market trends.

◈ **Create a financial crisis plan** – Pay off debts, secure emergency funds, and build multiple income sources.

◈ **Stockpile essentials** – Food, water, medicine, and alternative energy sources.

◈ **Invest wisely** – Consider hard assets like gold, silver, and real estate to hedge against economic uncertainty.

◈ **Build a support network** – A strong community is invaluable in times of crisis.

Final Thoughts

An economic collapse is not a spontaneous event—it is a process with clear warning signs. The key to surviving and thriving is **awareness and proactive preparation**. By recognizing these signs early and taking action, you can protect yourself, your family, and your assets from the devastating effects of financial disaster.

Chapter 2: The Best Assets to Own When the Economy Crashes

When an economic crisis hits, financial markets tumble, banks restrict access to money, and the cost of living skyrockets. If you're unprepared, your wealth can evaporate overnight. However, those who own **the right assets** can not only survive economic turmoil but also thrive during financial uncertainty.

In this chapter, we will explore the **best assets to own when the economy crashes**, how to diversify your holdings, and **how to build an emergency financial plan to safeguard your wealth during economic turmoil**.

The Characteristics of Crisis-Proof Assets

Before diving into specific asset classes, it's crucial to understand what makes an asset valuable during economic collapse. The best crisis-proof assets have the following qualities:

◈ **Tangible** – Physical assets retain value better than digital or paper assets.

◈ **Inflation-Proof** – Assets that hold value despite rising prices.

◈ **Widely Accepted** – Can be used for trade, barter, or conversion to needed resources.

◈ **Self-Sustaining** – Provides long-term utility, such as land that produces food.

◈ **Outside the Banking System** – Assets that are independent of government or financial institutions.

Now, let's explore **the best assets to own in a financial crisis**.

The Top 10 Best Assets to Own in an Economic Collapse

1. Precious Metals (Gold & Silver) – The Ultimate Crisis Currency

Gold and silver have been stores of value for thousands of years. Unlike paper money, which loses value during hyperinflation, precious metals remain valuable even in times of economic disaster.

Why Precious Metals Are Essential:

◈ Gold retains its value during financial crises.
◈ Silver is more practical for everyday trade and bartering.
◈ Both metals are **tangible and liquid**—easily sold or traded.

◈ **How to Invest Wisely:**

- Buy **physical** gold and silver, such as bullion coins or bars (not paper ETFs).
- Store metals in a **secure location** outside of banks.
- Avoid numismatic (collector) coins—stick to investment-grade gold and silver.

2. Cash (In Multiple Currencies) – Liquidity Is Power

During an economic collapse, **cash is king**—at least in the short term. When banks restrict withdrawals and digital transactions fail, physical cash allows you to buy necessary supplies.

Why Cash Matters:

◈ Immediate liquidity when digital payments fail.

◈ Essential for purchasing goods when banks limit withdrawals.

◈ Holding multiple currencies protects against a single currency collapse.

◈ **How to Store Cash:**

- Keep **3-6 months' worth** of living expenses in cash.
- Store in **multiple currencies** (U.S. dollars, Swiss francs, gold-backed currencies).
- Diversify locations (home safe, trusted family member, secured vault).

3. Real Estate and Land – Tangible Wealth Protection

While housing markets may fluctuate, land and real estate always have **intrinsic value**. Properties that generate income (rental properties, farmland) are especially valuable.

Why Real Estate Matters:

◈ Unlike paper money, real estate holds **long-term value**.

◈ Provides a **place to live** or **a source of income** during economic instability.

◈ **Farmland** offers self-sufficiency (food security, water access).

◈ **How to Invest Wisely:**

- Buy **productive land** (farmland, timberland, rental properties).
- Avoid high-debt properties that require large mortgage payments.
- If possible, **own land outright** to avoid foreclosure risks.

4. Food and Water Supplies – The Most Valuable Barter Asset

When supply chains break down, **food shortages** become a major crisis. Having **a stockpile of non-perishable food and access to clean water** is crucial.

Why Food & Water Matter:

◈ Food shortages lead to skyrocketing prices.
◈ Essential for survival—food is always in demand.
◈ Can be used for **bartering** in an economic collapse.

◈ **How to Prepare:**

- Stockpile **at least 6-12 months' worth** of food (rice, beans, canned goods, freeze-dried meals).
- Invest in **water purification systems** and store large water supplies.
- Grow your own food—consider building a **self-sustaining garden or greenhouse**.

5. Alternative Currencies (Cryptocurrency & Barter Items)

While traditional banking systems may fail, **alternative currencies** like Bitcoin and barterable goods can provide economic resilience.

Why Cryptocurrency Matters:

◈ Decentralized—outside of government control.
◈ Can be stored securely and accessed anywhere.
◈ Useful for international transactions.

◈ **How to Invest Wisely:**

- Store crypto in **cold wallets** (offline) to protect from cyberattacks.
- Prioritize **established cryptocurrencies** (Bitcoin, Ethereum) over risky altcoins.
- Keep a balance between **digital and tangible assets**.

6. Self-Defense Tools and Security

During economic collapses, crime rates **increase drastically** due to desperation. Having self-defense tools and security measures in place is critical.

Why Security Matters:

◈ Protects your family and assets from looters.

◈ Essential for securing food, water, and other supplies.

◈ Can be used for barter in extreme scenarios.

◈ **How to Prepare:**

- Invest in **home security** (reinforced doors, alarm systems, motion sensors).
- Consider **self-defense training**.
- Have **non-lethal** and **lethal** defense options (pepper spray, firearms where legal).

7. Essential Skills and Knowledge

Not all assets are physical—**skills are recession-proof** and can generate income even when traditional jobs disappear.

Most Valuable Survival Skills:

◈ Medical training (first aid, herbal medicine).

◈ Self-sufficiency (gardening, food preservation, mechanical repair).

◈ Defense training and situational awareness.

◈ **How to Prepare:**

- Take **first aid courses** and learn **basic medical care**.
- Develop practical trade skills (carpentry, plumbing, electrical work).
- Network with like-minded individuals to **trade skills for resources**.

How to Build an Emergency Financial Plan for Economic Collapse

Recognizing the best assets to own is only part of the solution. You also need an **actionable plan** to safeguard your wealth before a crisis strikes.

Step 1: Create a Financial Safety Net

◈ Save **at least 6-12 months' worth** of living expenses in **multiple currencies**.

◈ Store cash in **multiple locations** (home, trusted family, safe deposit box).

Step 2: Eliminate Debt

◈ Pay off **high-interest debt** first (credit cards, loans).

◈ Avoid new debt—**own assets outright** when possible.

Step 3: Diversify Investments

◈ Hold a **mix of cash, precious metals, real estate, and alternative currencies**.

◈ Keep essential goods (**food, medical supplies, water purification**) as part of your "wealth."

Step 4: Generate Multiple Income Streams

◈ Consider **recession-proof side businesses** (repair work, farming, online services).

◈ Invest in **income-generating assets** (rental properties, dividend stocks).

Step 5: Establish a Survival Network

◈ Connect with **like-minded people** who specialize in key survival skills.

◈ Build **barter networks** to trade goods and services **without relying on traditional money**.

Final Thoughts: The Future Belongs to the Prepared

Economic collapses are devastating for the unprepared but **opportunities** for those who anticipate them. By investing in **the right assets, securing financial independence, and developing valuable skills**, you can **thrive while others struggle**.

Chapter 3: The Role of Cryptocurrency in Financial Survival

Economic collapse often leads to failing banks, devalued fiat currency, and restricted access to financial resources. In such scenarios, traditional financial systems become unreliable, making alternative currencies like **cryptocurrency** an attractive option for safeguarding wealth and maintaining purchasing power.

In this chapter, we will explore:

- **How cryptocurrency can protect your wealth during economic turmoil**
- **Which cryptocurrencies offer the best security and stability**
- **How to safely store and use cryptocurrency in a financial crisis**
- **How to generate income during an economic collapse—even when jobs disappear and traditional markets crumble**

Why Cryptocurrency Matters in Economic Collapse

Unlike traditional fiat currencies controlled by governments and banks, **cryptocurrency operates on decentralized networks**, making it immune to inflation, banking restrictions, and political interference.

Key Benefits of Cryptocurrency During Economic Collapse

◈ **Decentralization** – No central authority can seize, freeze, or devalue your funds.

◈ **Inflation Resistance** – Cryptos like Bitcoin have a fixed supply, unlike fiat money that governments can print endlessly.

◈ **Portability and Accessibility** – Cryptocurrency can be accessed and transferred **anywhere in the world** without needing a bank.

◈ **Security and Anonymity** – Transactions can be private, protecting users from government overreach.

◈ **Borderless Transactions** – Can be used internationally without relying on foreign exchange rates.

During hyperinflation or a banking collapse, citizens often lose access to savings or find that **their money no longer holds value**. This has already happened in Venezuela, Zimbabwe, and Argentina—where people turned to **Bitcoin and stablecoins** to preserve their wealth and continue making transactions.

Which Cryptocurrencies Are Best for Economic Survival?

Not all cryptocurrencies are useful in a crisis. Some are **volatile**, while others have real-world stability. The best cryptos for economic survival include:

1. **Bitcoin (BTC) – The Digital Gold**

Bitcoin is the **most trusted cryptocurrency** and serves as a hedge against inflation.
◈ Scarce supply (only **21 million BTC** will ever exist).
◈ Recognized and accepted worldwide.
◈ Can be used as a store of value in unstable economies.

◈ **Survival Tip:** Buy Bitcoin in small amounts **before a crisis** and store it safely in an offline wallet.

2. Stablecoins (USDT, USDC, DAI) – Crypto Versions of Cash

Stablecoins are tied to real-world assets like the **U.S. dollar**, making them much **less volatile** than Bitcoin.
◈ Maintain **stable value** regardless of market fluctuations.
◈ Can be easily exchanged for goods and services.
◈ Provide an **alternative to failing fiat currencies**.

◈ **Survival Tip:** Convert some savings into **USDC or DAI** to preserve purchasing power if your national currency collapses.

3. Monero (XMR) – The Privacy Coin

Monero is a **fully anonymous** cryptocurrency, making it **ideal for privacy-conscious users**.
◈ Transactions are **untraceable**, preventing government tracking.
◈ Secure from seizures or restrictions.
◈ Useful in regions where financial surveillance is high.

◈ **Survival Tip:** If governments impose strict financial controls, Monero can be used for **private transactions** without detection.

4. Ethereum (ETH) – The Smart Contract King

Ethereum is more than just a currency—it powers **decentralized applications (dApps)**, which can provide financial tools **outside the traditional banking system**.

◈ Can be used for **secure, borderless transactions**.

◈ Smart contracts allow decentralized finance (DeFi) transactions.

◈ Offers opportunities to **earn passive income** through staking.

◈ **Survival Tip:** If banks collapse, DeFi platforms on Ethereum can still provide loans and financial services.

How to Safely Store and Use Cryptocurrency in an Economic Collapse

Owning cryptocurrency is only **one part of the equation**. You must also know **how to store, secure, and access your crypto safely** in a crisis.

1. Use Cold Storage (Offline Wallets)

Storing crypto in **exchange wallets (like Binance, Coinbase, or Kraken)** is risky because:

◈ Governments can seize assets from centralized exchanges.
◈ Banks and payment processors can **freeze withdrawals**.
◈ Hackers frequently target **online wallets**.

◈ **Solution:** Move your crypto to a **hardware wallet (Ledger, Trezor)** or a **paper wallet**.

2. Keep Backups of Wallet Keys

◈ If you lose your **private key or recovery phrase**, you will lose access to your crypto.
◈ Store backups in multiple **secure locations** (physical safe, encrypted USB drive, hidden written copy).

3. Learn How to Use Peer-to-Peer (P2P) Transactions

If banks collapse, **crypto exchanges may become inaccessible**. You must know how to:

◈ Trade Bitcoin or stablecoins **directly with others**.
◈ Use decentralized exchanges (**Uniswap, PancakeSwap**) instead of centralized platforms.

◈ **Survival Tip:** Practice **small P2P transactions** before a crisis so you're comfortable using them.

How to Generate Income with Cryptocurrency During Economic Collapse

When traditional jobs disappear, **crypto offers alternative income sources**. Here's how:

1. Freelancing and Remote Work (Paid in Crypto)

◈ Work as a **writer, programmer, designer, consultant**, or any digital job.
◈ Get paid in **Bitcoin, Ethereum, or stablecoins**.
◈ Use platforms like **Bitwage, Cryptogrind, or Upwork (with crypto payments)**.

◈ **Survival Tip:** Offer services that people still need **even in a financial crisis**—such as survival planning, alternative healthcare, or repair work.

2. Peer-to-Peer (P2P) Trading

◈ Buy Bitcoin/crypto at a low price and **resell at a profit**.
◈ Trade goods and services for **crypto payments**.
◈ Use platforms like **LocalBitcoins or Paxful**.

◈ **Survival Tip:** In an economic crash, cash may become **scarce**, but crypto can remain valuable for trade.

3. Crypto Staking & Yield Farming

◈ Earn passive income by **staking crypto** on platforms like Ethereum, Polkadot, or Tezos.
◈ Yield farming allows you to lend crypto **in exchange for interest payments**.

◈ **Survival Tip:** Only stake **a portion** of your crypto so you always have liquid funds.

4. Crypto-Backed Loans

◈ Use crypto as **collateral** to take out loans **without using a bank**.
◈ Platforms like **Aave, Compound, and MakerDAO** allow users to borrow **without credit checks**.

◈ **Survival Tip:** If you're in a **cash emergency**, you can get a loan **without selling your Bitcoin**.

5. Accepting Crypto Payments for Business

◈ Set up **crypto payment options** for an online or local business.
◈ Accept payments in **Bitcoin, Monero, or stablecoins** for **bartering and trade**.

◈ **Survival Tip:** Businesses that accept **crypto payments** can bypass failing banking systems.

Final Thoughts: Cryptocurrency as Your Economic Survival Tool

In times of economic collapse, those who **prepare and adapt** will thrive. **Cryptocurrency offers a decentralized, inflation-resistant financial tool** that allows you to store wealth, make transactions, and generate income when traditional systems fail.

Your Action Plan for Crypto Financial Survival:

◈ **Diversify your crypto holdings** – Bitcoin for long-term security, stablecoins for daily transactions, Monero for privacy.
◈ **Store crypto securely** – Use **cold wallets** and keep backup keys in multiple safe locations.
◈ **Learn P2P trading** – So you can **buy, sell, and exchange crypto without relying on banks**.
◈ **Develop crypto income streams** – Freelancing, staking, trading, and accepting payments in crypto.

Chapter 4: How to Build an Emergency Financial Plan

When an economic collapse strikes, financial stability vanishes almost overnight. Banks impose restrictions, inflation skyrockets, and essential goods become scarce. Without a well-structured **emergency financial plan**, you risk losing access to your money, food, and basic survival necessities.

In this chapter, we will **guide you through building an economic collapse-proof financial plan**, including:

- **How to safeguard your money before a financial disaster**
- **How to develop an alternative economy through bartering and community networks**
- **How to secure resources that will remain valuable even if cash becomes worthless**
- **How to ensure long-term financial survival**

The Core Elements of an Economic Collapse-Proof Financial Plan

A **strong financial survival plan** consists of:

⟐ **Emergency Savings & Cash Reserves** – Short-term liquidity in case banks limit withdrawals.

⟐ **Inflation-Proof Assets** – Investments that retain value even as fiat currency collapses.

⟐ **Income Diversification** – Multiple ways to earn money outside traditional jobs.

⟐ **Essential Supplies & Barter Items** – Physical assets that can be traded.

⟐ **Community Networks & Support Systems** – Reliable connections for trade and survival.

Let's break each of these down into **actionable steps**.

Step 1: Safeguard Your Cash & Savings Before a Crisis

1. Keep Emergency Cash Outside of Banks

Banks are vulnerable in economic collapses, often restricting withdrawals or even freezing accounts. To avoid losing access to your money:

◈ Store at least **3-6 months' worth** of living expenses in **physical cash**.

◈ Keep small bills ($1s, $5s, $10s) for easier transactions.

◈ Hide cash in multiple secure locations (**home safe, hidden compartments, family members you trust**).

◈ **Survival Tip:** Don't store all your wealth in one place. Diversify locations in case of theft or emergency.

2. Diversify Your Currency Holdings

In case the national currency collapses, holding alternative currencies can protect your purchasing power.

◈ Hold **multiple currencies** (e.g., U.S. dollars, Swiss francs, Euros).

◈ Keep **stablecoins (USDT, USDC, DAI)** as digital alternatives to fiat.

◈ Store **precious metals (gold, silver)** as a long-term hedge against inflation.

◈ **Survival Tip:** If hyperinflation hits, foreign currencies and stablecoins may hold value better than local cash.

Step 2: Invest in Inflation-Proof Assets

During an economic collapse, **traditional investments (stocks, bonds, retirement accounts)** often lose value. Instead, shift your focus to **tangible assets that hold value no matter what happens**.

Best Inflation-Proof Assets:

◈ **Gold & Silver** – Reliable store of value for thousands of years.

◈ **Real Estate & Land** – Provides housing, rental income, or farming potential.

◈ **Cryptocurrency (Bitcoin, Monero, Stablecoins)** – Alternative wealth storage outside of banking systems.

◈ **Food & Water Supplies** – Always in demand during financial crises.

◈ **Survival Tip:** Convert **a portion of your savings** into these assets before a collapse hits.

Step 3: Create Multiple Income Streams for Long-Term Survival

If your **primary job disappears** in a crisis, you need **alternative income sources** to survive.

How to Build Multiple Income Streams:

◈ **Start a side business** – Repair work, farming, tutoring, writing, or self-defense training.

◈ **Sell essential goods** – Stockpile barterable items and trade them for cash or other goods.

◈ **Offer remote services** – Work online in fields like consulting, digital marketing, and IT.

◈ **Leverage crypto earnings** – Staking, trading, and accepting crypto for services.

◈ **Survival Tip:** The more income streams you have, the **less dependent you are on a single failing economy**.

Step 4: Stockpile Essential Supplies & Bartering Goods

In a financial crisis, cash may become **worthless**, but tangible goods **always** retain value. A solid financial survival plan includes a **barter system** for acquiring and trading essential goods.

Best Barter Items to Stockpile:

◈ **Food & Water** – Canned goods, rice, beans, freeze-dried meals.

◈ **Medical Supplies** – First aid kits, painkillers, antibiotics, bandages.

◈ **Fuel & Energy Sources** – Propane, batteries, solar chargers, firewood.

◈ **Personal Hygiene Products** – Soap, toothpaste, toilet paper, feminine hygiene items.

◈ **Alcohol & Tobacco** – Always valuable for trade.

◈ **Tools & Hardware** – Hand tools, knives, sewing kits, rope, duct tape.

◈ **Ammunition & Firearms** – Essential for defense and trade (where legal).

◈ **Survival Tip:** If the economy collapses, **barter replaces money**. Stockpile **small, tradable items** for everyday exchanges.

Step 5: Build a Strong Community & Barter Network

Surviving a financial collapse is **easier with a reliable network**. Establish relationships with **local farmers, skilled workers, and trade partners** to create a **self-sufficient barter economy**.

How to Build a Barter Network:

◈ **Connect with like-minded individuals** – Join survivalist groups, farming co-ops, and barter clubs.

◈ **Develop useful skills** – Learning **plumbing, medical care, or mechanics** makes you valuable in a trade economy.

◈ **Create a barter agreement** – Work out **fair exchanges of goods and services** before a crisis escalates.

◈ **Form mutual aid groups** – A **tight-knit community** offers protection, food, and labor-sharing benefits.

◈ **Survival Tip: Trading skills is just as valuable as trading goods**. Learn **self-reliance skills that others will need** in a crisis.

Step 6: Secure Alternative Energy & Shelter Options

Power grids and housing markets are **vulnerable** during economic collapse. Having **backup energy and alternative shelter** ensures **long-term survival**.

◈ **Invest in solar panels** – A renewable **off-grid** energy source.

◈ **Stockpile fuel** – Gasoline, propane, firewood, and diesel.

◈ **Consider mobile shelter options** – RVs, tiny homes, or cabins **offer flexibility if relocation is necessary**.

◈ **Strengthen home security** – Upgrade locks, install security cameras, and prepare for possible looters.

◈ **Survival Tip:** Economic turmoil increases crime—**home security and alternative sheltering plans are crucial**.

Finalizing Your Economic Collapse-Proof Financial Plan

A well-rounded financial survival plan is **more than just having cash**—it's about securing **long-term sustainability**.

Final Checklist for an Economic Collapse-Proof Plan:

◈ **Cash Savings** – 3-6 months of expenses in small bills.

◈ **Hard Assets** – Gold, silver, land, tools, and other tangible goods.

◈ **Multiple Income Streams** – Freelancing, bartering, essential services.

◈ **Essential Supplies** – Food, water, medical, hygiene, and fuel.

◈ **Barter Network** – Trusted contacts for trading goods and services.

◈ **Energy Independence** – Backup power sources, alternative shelter.

◈ **Security & Self-Defense** – Protect yourself, your home, and your assets.

◈ **Survival Tip:** Start preparing **now**—don't wait until an economic collapse is already in motion.

Final Thoughts: Survive and Thrive in a Financial Crisis

While economic collapses are unpredictable, **they are inevitable** at some point. The key to **thriving instead of suffering** is **preparation**.

By creating a **comprehensive financial survival plan**, investing in **alternative assets**, and **building a barter economy**, you can **secure your future** even in the worst financial disasters.

Chapter 5: Off-Grid Living: A Financial Safety Net

Economic collapses bring uncertainty—markets crash, inflation spirals out of control, jobs disappear, and essential services like food, water, and healthcare become unreliable. The best way to **guarantee long-term survival** and **financial independence** is to remove yourself from the vulnerabilities of failing systems. This is where **off-grid living** comes in.

This chapter will explore:

- **How off-grid living acts as a financial safety net**
- **How to achieve self-sufficiency through food production**
- **Alternative power solutions to survive without reliance on the grid**
- **Medical independence to maintain health and well-being in a crisis**

By the end of this chapter, you will have a clear roadmap for **living independently**, free from reliance on unstable economies, supply chains, and government support.

Why Off-Grid Living is the Ultimate Financial Safety Net

Off-grid living means **creating a self-sustaining lifestyle that doesn't rely on external systems like banks, grocery stores, or utility companies**. This approach is crucial in an economic collapse because:

◈ **Food prices skyrocket** – If you grow your own food, you're insulated from inflation.

◈ **Power grids fail** – If you have solar or alternative energy, blackouts won't affect you.

◈ **Medical costs rise** – If you practice self-sufficient healthcare, you won't need expensive treatments.

◈ **Crime increases** – If you live in a secure off-grid location, you reduce the risk of looting and violence.

◈ **Survival Tip:** The less you rely on failing institutions, the better your chances of surviving and even thriving when the economy collapses.

Step 1: Building a Self-Sufficient Food Supply

Food security is the **foundation of off-grid survival**. A self-sufficient food system ensures you have **a renewable food source**, regardless of economic instability.

1. Growing Your Own Food (Gardening & Permaculture)

◈ Start a **survival garden** with high-calorie, nutrient-rich crops:

- **Staple crops** – Potatoes, beans, corn, squash, and root vegetables.
- **Leafy greens** – Spinach, kale, Swiss chard (nutrient-dense, fast-growing).
- **Fruit trees** – Apples, pears, berries (perennial food sources).

◈ Use **permaculture principles** to create a **low-maintenance** food system:

- **Companion planting** – Grow crops that benefit each other (e.g., corn, beans, and squash together).
- **Hugelkultur gardening** – Retains moisture and nutrients without fertilizers.
- **Rainwater irrigation** – Capture and store rainwater for irrigation.

◈ **Survival Tip:** Start your **off-grid food production NOW**—don't wait until a crisis to learn how to grow food.

2. Raising Livestock for Sustainable Protein

Meat, dairy, and eggs provide **high-protein, sustainable food sources**. The best options for an off-grid lifestyle include:

◈ **Chickens** – Provide eggs and meat; easy to raise.
◈ **Goats** – Produce milk and meat; require little space.
◈ **Rabbits** – High-yield meat source; fast reproduction.
◈ **Fish Farming (Aquaponics)** – Sustainable protein source using minimal water.

◈ **Survival Tip:** Choose **low-maintenance livestock** that thrive on **natural forage** and require minimal supplemental feed.

3. Preserving and Storing Food for Long-Term Use

◈ **Canning** – Store fruits, vegetables, and meats without refrigeration.
◈ **Dehydrating** – Dry fruits, vegetables, and herbs for long-term storage.
◈ **Root cellaring** – Store root vegetables, squash, and apples naturally.
◈ **Fermentation** – Extend shelf life while maintaining probiotics (e.g., sauerkraut, kimchi).

◈ **Survival Tip:** Stockpile at least **1 year's worth of preserved food** to prepare for bad growing seasons.

Step 2: Alternative Power Solutions for Energy Independence

Utility companies become **unreliable or unaffordable** in economic turmoil. Off-grid energy solutions give you **independence from power grid failures and high electricity costs.**

1. Solar Power – The Most Reliable Off-Grid Energy Source

◈ Invest in **solar panels** to generate electricity.
◈ Use **deep-cycle batteries** to store power for nighttime use.
◈ Set up **solar-powered appliances** (refrigerators, lights, fans).

◈ **Survival Tip:** Learn to install and maintain solar panels **yourself** to avoid relying on contractors.

2. Wind & Hydroelectric Power

◈ **Wind turbines** – Effective in areas with consistent wind speeds.
◈ **Micro-hydro generators** – Ideal for properties near running water.
◈ **Hybrid systems** – Combine solar, wind, and hydro for **maximum energy security.**

◈ **Survival Tip:** Diversify energy sources so you aren't dependent on just **one** type of power.

3. Low-Tech Energy Solutions for Daily Use

◈ **Wood-burning stoves** – Provide heat and cooking abilities.
◈ **Hand-crank radios and flashlights** – No electricity needed.
◈ **Solar ovens** – Cook food without using fuel or electricity.
◈ **Gravity-fed water filtration systems** – Clean water without electricity.

◈ **Survival Tip:** Keep **backup energy sources** for when solar power is unavailable (e.g., stormy days).

Step 3: Medical Independence – Health Without a Hospital

In an economic collapse, **hospitals may become overcrowded, expensive, or unavailable.** Learning **basic medical self-sufficiency** is essential.

1. Stockpiling Essential Medical Supplies

◈ First aid kits (**bandages, antiseptics, gauze, sutures**).

◈ Over-the-counter meds (**pain relievers, anti-diarrhea, antihistamines**).

◈ Prescription medications (**if possible, get extra supplies in advance**).

◈ **Survival Tip:** Store antibiotics (fish antibiotics are often identical to human versions).

2. Learning Herbal & Alternative Medicine

◈ **Grow medicinal plants** (garlic, ginger, turmeric, echinacea).

◈ **Learn herbal remedies** for infections, pain relief, and wound care.

◈ **Practice holistic healthcare** (meditation, acupuncture, fasting).

◈ **Survival Tip:** Invest in books and training courses on **herbal medicine and alternative healthcare.**

3. Preventive Healthcare & Physical Fitness

◈ **Exercise regularly** – Strength and endurance matter in survival situations.

◈ **Eat clean, nutrient-dense foods** to prevent disease.

◈ **Learn stress management** – Mental resilience is as important as physical health.

◈ **Survival Tip:** The healthier you are, the **less you rely on the medical system.**

Finalizing Your Off-Grid Survival Plan

Final Checklist for Off-Grid Financial Independence:

◈ **Self-Sufficient Food System** – Gardening, livestock, food preservation.

◈ **Alternative Power Sources** – Solar, wind, hydro, low-tech energy solutions.

◈ **Medical Independence** – First aid, herbal medicine, stockpiling supplies.

◈ **Security & Defense** – Protecting your property and resources.

◈ **Water Supply & Filtration** – Wells, rain collection, purification systems.

◈ **Survival Tip:** The **goal of off-grid living is complete self-reliance**—every step you take toward independence reduces your dependence on unstable economies.

Final Thoughts: Off-Grid Living is Your Economic Shield

While an economic collapse can **wipe out wealth, those who live off-grid remain secure**. By producing **your own food, generating your own power, and maintaining your own health**, you can **thrive even in the worst financial disasters**.

Chapter 6: How to Recession-Proof Your Income

Economic recessions and collapses devastate personal finances—jobs disappear, wages stagnate, and businesses shut down. Those who **fail to prepare** often find themselves struggling with no reliable income, sky-rocketing costs, and increasing financial stress.

This chapter will teach you:

◈ **How to create multiple streams of income to withstand an economic downturn**

◈ **How to build recession-proof businesses and side hustles**

◈ **How to prepare for economic collapse in an urban setting** so you can survive even if you can't go fully off-grid

◈ **How to invest wisely and protect your purchasing power**

If you take action now, you won't just survive the next financial crisis—you'll **thrive** while others struggle.

Why Recession-Proofing Your Income is Essential

The job market **collapses first** in an economic downturn. Businesses cut costs, automation replaces workers, and industries shrink due to lower consumer spending. Those who rely on a **single paycheck** or a **single industry** are most at risk.

◈ **Survival Truth:** The more **income streams** you have, the **less vulnerable** you are to financial collapse.

Warning Signs of Job Market Collapse:

◈ **Mass layoffs** in major industries (tech, manufacturing, retail, transportation).

◈ **Hiring freezes**—companies stop adding new employees.

◈ **Wage stagnation**—pay doesn't increase even as inflation rises.

◈ **More competition for fewer jobs**—job postings get thousands of applicants.

◈ **Recession-Proof Plan: Before** a collapse, start securing multiple income sources so you are never **fully dependent on one employer.**

Step 1: Diversifying Your Income – The Golden Rule of Financial Survival

◈ **Never rely on a single source of income.**

◈ **Always have multiple streams of cash flow**—so if one disappears, others still provide financial security.

The best **recession-proof income sources** include:

1. Freelancing and Remote Work

◈ Provides flexibility and **income even if local businesses shut down**.

◈ Allows you to **earn money internationally**, bypassing currency collapses.

Best Freelance Jobs:

- Writing & Copywriting
- Graphic Design
- Video Editing
- Social Media Management
- Programming & Web Development
- Virtual Assistance

◈ **Survival Tip:** Sign up for **Upwork, Fiverr, PeoplePerHour, or Toptal** and start offering services **before** a financial crisis hits.

2. Starting an Online Business (E-Commerce & Digital Products)

◈ Selling online means you can **reach customers worldwide**, even in a recession.

◈ Digital products and online courses **generate passive income** with minimal cost.

Best Online Businesses for Economic Survival:

- Print-on-demand (T-shirts, mugs, home decor).
- Selling digital products (ebooks, templates, guides).
- Online tutoring or coaching.
- Dropshipping (sell products without keeping inventory).
- Affiliate marketing (earn money recommending products).

◈ **Survival Tip:** Build an online store on **Shopify, Etsy, Gumroad, or Amazon KDP** to create an automated income stream.

3. Investing in Recession-Proof Assets

◈ **Investments that don't lose value in a crisis** help you **preserve** wealth.

Best Recession-Proof Investments:

- **Gold & Silver** – Protects against inflation and currency collapse.
- **Real Estate** – Rental income remains valuable during economic downturns.
- **Dividend Stocks** – Companies that **pay consistent dividends** generate income even in a recession.
- **Cryptocurrency (Bitcoin, Stablecoins, Monero)** – Protects wealth **outside the banking system.**

◈ **Survival Tip:** Focus on **cash-flow investments** that generate **monthly income**, rather than stocks that depend on selling later.

4. Building a Side Hustle that Works in Any Economy

◈ Having **a small business or service-based income** keeps money flowing in tough times.

Best Side Hustles for Recession-Proofing:

- **Repair Services** – People still need appliances, cars, and homes fixed.
- **Personal Security & Self-Defense Training** – Crime rises in economic downturns.
- **Gardening & Urban Farming** – Sell homegrown food or start a CSA (Community Supported Agriculture).
- **Medical and First Aid Training** – Offer CPR or survival medicine courses.
- **Reselling Goods** – Buy used or discounted products and sell for profit.

◈ **Survival Tip: Start small now**—refine your skills and build a **customer base** before economic conditions get worse.

Step 2: Preparing for Economic Collapse in an Urban Setting

Even if you can't move off-grid, you can still **reduce your financial risks** and **protect yourself** in a city or suburb.

1. Reduce Dependency on Fragile Systems

◈ **Stockpile essentials** – Food, water, medical supplies, and hygiene products.

◈ **Have alternative power solutions** – Portable solar panels, generators, power banks.

◈ **Secure transportation** – Bicycles, public transport alternatives, fuel reserves.

◈ **Survival Tip:** Create a **network of like-minded people** for support and bartering.

2. Develop a Bartering System for Urban Survival

◈ If cash becomes worthless, **bartering replaces money**.

◈ Trade **skills and supplies** to get what you need.

Best Barter Items in an Economic Collapse:

- Food & Water Purification Supplies
- First Aid & Medical Supplies
- Batteries, Fuel, & Alternative Energy Sources
- Weapons & Ammunition
- Hygiene Products

◈ **Survival Tip:** Build a **community barter network** where **people exchange goods & services instead of relying on cash.**

3. Protect Your Home & Assets from Crime & Looters

◈ Crime **increases dramatically** during economic collapses.

◈ Secure your home **before** law enforcement becomes unreliable.

Urban Security Tips:

◈ Install **reinforced doors, security cameras, and motion sensors**.

◈ Use **window reinforcements** to prevent break-ins.

◈ Have **non-lethal self-defense tools** (pepper spray, batons, tasers).

◈ If legal, **consider firearms** for home defense.

◈ **Survival Tip:** Join **neighborhood watch groups** or create a **local defense network** with trusted individuals.

4. Learn Essential Urban Survival Skills

◈ **Cooking without electricity** – Use solar cookers or rocket stoves.

◈ **Finding clean water** – Learn rainwater collection and urban water filtration.

◈ **Navigating power outages** – Have backup energy sources like hand-crank radios and power banks.

◈ **Survival Tip:** Even **small-scale self-sufficiency** (a rooftop garden, food storage, energy backups) helps **reduce reliance on collapsing systems**.

Step 3: Build a Long-Term Survival Income Plan

The best financial survival plans **aren't just about making money—they ensure you can survive indefinitely, no matter what happens.**

Final Checklist for Recession-Proofing Your Income:

◈ **At least three sources of income** – Freelancing, side business, investments.

◈ **Passive income streams** – Digital products, rental income, dividends.

◈ **Cash & crisis-proof investments** – Gold, silver, real estate, cryptocurrency.

◈ **Stockpiled essentials** – Food, medical supplies, barterable goods.

◈ **Urban survival skills** – Water purification, security, bartering.

◈ **Survival Tip: Start recession-proofing today**—once an economic collapse is underway, it will be **too late** to secure income and resources.

Final Thoughts: Survive & Prosper in Any Economy

An economic downturn doesn't mean **financial ruin**—it means **new opportunities** for those who are prepared. By **diversifying your income, securing assets, and building urban survival strategies**, you can protect yourself from **financial disaster**.

Chapter 7: The Psychology of Staying Calm During a Financial Crisis

Economic collapses create **panic, fear, and uncertainty**, leading many people to **make rash decisions** that worsen their situation. However, those who **stay calm and think strategically** can **protect their wealth, secure essential resources, and even thrive** while others struggle.

This chapter will cover:

◈ **How to develop a resilient mindset in financial crises**

◈ **How to control fear and avoid emotional decision-making**

◈ **How to protect your wealth during hyperinflation**—where to store money, what to invest in, and how to avoid losing everything when currency becomes worthless

◈ **How to make smart financial and survival choices under stress**

By mastering the **psychology of financial survival**, you will stay ahead of the crisis and **turn panic into preparation**.

The Psychological Impact of a Financial Crisis

When the economy collapses, the **emotional response** is often more dangerous than the actual event. Fear leads to:

◈ **Panic selling** – People dump assets at the worst possible time.

◈ **Bank runs** – Mass withdrawals crash financial institutions.

◈ **Hoarding behaviors** – Supermarkets and supply chains collapse due to sudden demand spikes.

◈ **Poor financial decisions** – People buy into scams, overpay for supplies, or go into extreme debt.

Why Staying Calm is the Key to Survival

Those who **remain rational and proactive** during a crisis can:

◈ Secure their finances **before** inflation wipes out savings.
◈ Invest in **real assets** that hold value.
◈ Prepare **long before shortages happen**.
◈ Stay mentally strong while others collapse under stress.

◈ **Survival Truth: Mental resilience is just as important as financial preparation.**

Step 1: How to Stay Mentally Strong in a Financial Collapse

1. Shift Your Mindset from Fear to Strategy

◈ Replace **fear-based thinking** with **strategic decision-making**.
◈ Ask yourself: *"What is in my control, and what actions can I take today?"*
◈ Recognize that **all economic collapses create opportunities** for those who prepare.

◈ **Survival Tip:** Focus on **solutions, not problems**—every crisis has a **path forward**.

2. Avoid Media-Induced Panic

◈ **News outlets thrive on fear**—limit exposure to **doom-and-gloom reporting**.
◈ Stick to **factual financial reports**, not emotional headlines.
◈ Follow **trusted economists, not social media rumors**.

◈ **Survival Tip:** Stay informed, but **don't let fear drive your financial decisions**.

3. Develop a Crisis Routine

◈ **Create a daily routine** to maintain control over your life.
◈ Focus on **income-generating activities, learning survival skills, and networking**.
◈ Stay **physically active**—exercise reduces stress and improves decision-making.

◈ **Survival Tip: Control what you can**—small actions daily prevent panic from taking over.

Step 2: How to Protect Your Wealth During Hyperinflation

Hyperinflation occurs when **money loses value rapidly**, making everyday essentials unaffordable.

How Hyperinflation Destroys Savings:

◈ Prices **double or triple in days or weeks.**

◈ Savings accounts **become worthless** as currency collapses.

◈ Governments **freeze bank accounts or limit withdrawals.**

◈ Essentials like **food, water, and medicine become the new currency.**

◈ **Survival Truth: Money isn't real wealth—real assets are.**

Where to Store Money to Protect Against Hyperinflation

1. Convert Cash Into Hard Assets

◈ **Gold & Silver** – Historically retains value even when currencies collapse.

◈ **Land & Real Estate** – Physical property is always in demand.

◈ **Food & Essential Supplies** – In hyperinflation, **necessities become more valuable than cash.**

◈ **Survival Tip: Store wealth in physical, tradable assets**, not paper money.

2. Hold Foreign Currencies & Cryptocurrencies

◈ **Diversify into stable foreign currencies** – Swiss francs, U.S. dollars, Singapore dollars.

◈ **Cryptocurrency (Bitcoin, Monero, Stablecoins)** – A hedge against fiat currency collapse.

◈ **Store crypto in offline wallets** to protect against cyberattacks.

◈ **Survival Tip:** Keep cash **outside failing banking systems**—many governments freeze withdrawals during financial crises.

3. Invest in Inflation-Proof Assets

◈ **Dividend-Paying Stocks** – Companies that pay cash dividends retain value better than paper money.

◈ **Commodities (Oil, Natural Gas, Agriculture)** – Always in demand.

◈ **Productive Farmland** – Provides **food security and wealth storage**.

◈ **Survival Tip:** If the economy collapses, **you want assets that people need, not just paper money.**

4. Build a Bartering & Trade Economy

◈ **Cash loses value, but bartering thrives.**

◈ Stockpile **high-demand trade items**:

- Food & Water Purification
- Medical & First Aid Supplies
- Ammunition & Self-Defense Tools
- Fuel & Batteries
- Alcohol & Cigarettes (highly tradeable in crises)

◈ **Survival Tip:** Money may become useless—**trade networks will replace currency.**

Step 3: How to Avoid Financial Disaster in a Crisis

1. Get Out of Debt Before the Collapse

◈ Inflation makes debt **unmanageable** as interest rates spike.

◈ Avoid credit card debt, **adjustable-rate mortgages**, and high-interest loans.

◈ If possible, **pay off debt early or switch to fixed-rate loans.**

◈ **Survival Tip:** The less debt you have, the **more financial control you maintain.**

2. Create an Emergency Financial Plan

◈ **Save 3-6 months' worth of expenses in multiple currencies.**

◈ **Secure assets in diversified locations** (home safe, vaults, offshore accounts).

◈ **Develop multiple income streams** – Don't rely on one job or business.

◈ **Survival Tip:** Prepare **before the crisis hits**—once hyperinflation starts, **it's already too late.**

3. Know When to Pull Money Out of the Bank

◈ If **inflation is above 10-15%,** start withdrawing cash.

◈ Convert savings into **gold, real estate, food, and essential supplies.**

◈ Watch for **government-imposed banking restrictions**—withdrawals may be **limited or frozen.**

◈ **Survival Tip:** Keep only **minimal cash in banks**—the rest should be **stored in hard assets.**

4. Be Ready to Relocate if Necessary

◈ **Some countries handle financial crises better than others.**

◈ If conditions worsen, having **foreign assets or bank accounts** can provide an escape route.

◈ Learn about **residency or citizenship options in stable economies** (Switzerland, Singapore, Canada).

◈ **Survival Tip:** A **"Plan B" country** gives you options if economic collapse turns violent.

Finalizing Your Psychological & Financial Survival Plan

Final Checklist for Thriving in a Financial Crisis:

◈ **Master your emotions** – Fear leads to financial mistakes.
◈ **Diversify assets** – Gold, silver, real estate, food, and crypto.
◈ **Prepare for hyperinflation** – Hard assets, foreign currencies, bartering.
◈ **Avoid debt & banking risks** – Keep wealth outside fragile systems.
◈ **Develop multiple income streams** – Freelancing, investments, barter trade.

◈ **Survival Truth: The calmest minds make the best decisions**—panic only benefits those who manipulate the crisis.

Final Thoughts: The Strong Survive, The Smart Thrive

Financial disasters **are survivable**—but only for those who stay **mentally strong and strategically prepared**. By mastering the **psychology of financial crisis survival**, protecting your **wealth from hyperinflation**, and **adapting quickly**, you can turn crisis into opportunity.

Chapter 8: Alternative Investments That Hold Value in Hard Times

A financial collapse can wipe out savings, destroy traditional investments, and render paper money worthless. However, history has shown that those who **invest wisely in alternative assets** can not only **survive economic disasters** but **thrive in a post-collapse economy**.

In this chapter, we will cover:

◈ **Alternative investments that retain value during economic downturns**

◈ **How to protect your wealth from market crashes and currency collapses**

◈ **How to rebuild financial security and identify new investment opportunities**

◈ **How to turn a crisis into long-term prosperity**

While the unprepared panic, **those who invest in real, durable assets** will emerge stronger.

The Problem with Traditional Investments in a Collapse

Most people keep their wealth in **bank accounts, stocks, retirement funds, and paper currency**—all of which can be **wiped out in an economic collapse**.

Why Traditional Investments Fail in Hard Times:

◈ **Cash Loses Value Fast** – Hyperinflation makes savings worthless overnight.

◈ **Stock Markets Crash** – Stocks can lose 50-90% of their value in a crisis.

◈ **Banks Freeze Accounts** – Governments impose withdrawal limits or seize funds.

◈ **Retirement Funds Tank** – Pensions, 401(k)s, and IRAs become nearly worthless.

◈ **Survival Truth:** The safest investments in a crisis are **tangible, necessary, and independent of fragile financial systems**.

Best Alternative Investments for Economic Survival

To thrive in a post-collapse world, you must **shift your mindset from traditional investing to real-world wealth**.

1. Gold & Silver: The Ultimate Store of Value

◈ **Why It Works:** Precious metals retain value **regardless of currency collapse**.

◈ **Best For:** Storing wealth safely without reliance on banks.

◈ **How to Invest:** Buy **physical gold & silver coins or bars**, NOT ETFs or paper gold.

◈ **Survival Tip: Silver** is better for small transactions, while **gold** is best for preserving large amounts of wealth.

2. Real Estate & Land: Physical Wealth That Endures

◈ **Why It Works:** Unlike paper money, land and property retain **intrinsic value**.

◈ **Best For:** Generating income through **rent, farming, or barter**.

◈ **How to Invest:** Focus on **rural land, rental properties, and farmland**, NOT high-debt real estate.

◈ **Survival Tip:** A **self-sufficient property** (water, food production, energy sources) is one of the **best investments** in a crisis.

3. Farmland & Food Production: The Most Valuable Asset in a Crisis

◈ **Why It Works:** When food shortages hit, farmland becomes priceless.

◈ **Best For:** Producing your own food and selling/bartering surplus.

◈ **How to Invest:**

- Buy **fertile land** for growing crops or raising livestock.
- Set up **greenhouses or aquaponics** for year-round food supply.

◈ **Survival Tip:** Post-collapse economies revolve around **food security**—owning farmland gives you **power and wealth**.

4. Essential Commodities: Investing in Scarcity

◈ **Why It Works:** In a crisis, basic goods **become currency**.
◈ **Best For:** Bartering and resale for huge profits.
◈ **What to Stockpile:**

- **Food & Water** – Canned goods, rice, beans, freeze-dried meals.
- **Medical Supplies** – First aid kits, antibiotics, painkillers.
- **Fuel & Energy** – Propane, gasoline, solar power kits.
- **Ammunition & Firearms** – High-value trade items (where legal).

◈ **Survival Tip:** Store **small, tradable items**—people will pay **ANY price** for necessities in a crisis.

5. Cryptocurrency: The Digital Hedge Against Banking Failures

◈ **Why It Works:** Crypto operates **outside the traditional banking system**.
◈ **Best For:** Storing wealth without government interference.
◈ **How to Invest:**

- **Bitcoin (BTC)** – Digital gold for long-term wealth.
- **Monero (XMR)** – Private transactions shielded from government tracking.
- **Stablecoins (USDT, USDC, DAI)** – Hold value without inflation risks.

◈ **Survival Tip:** Keep crypto in **cold storage wallets**—don't rely on exchanges that might freeze accounts.

6. Self-Sufficiency Investments: The Wealth of Independence

⟐ **Why It Works:** The less you depend on failing systems, the more **financially secure** you are.

⟐ **Best For:** Reducing expenses and ensuring long-term survival.

⟐ **What to Invest In:**

- **Solar Panels & Alternative Energy** – Power independence.
- **Water Purification Systems** – Clean water without relying on public utilities.
- **Homesteading & DIY Tools** – Skills for self-sufficient living.

⟐ **Survival Tip:** Post-collapse, **skills & resources** become **more valuable than money**.

Thriving in a Post-Collapse Economy: Rebuilding Financial Security

A crisis destroys old economic systems but **creates new opportunities** for those who adapt.

How to Identify Investment Opportunities After a Collapse

⟐ **Rebuild Essential Services** – The best businesses post-collapse will be:

- Food production
- Water purification
- Alternative medicine
- Home security
- Barter & trade networks

⟐ **Control High-Demand Resources** – Anything people **need to survive** will be worth more than money.

⟐ **Start a Small Business Focused on Survival Essentials** – Teach, trade, or provide services people need.

◈ **Survival Tip:** The post-collapse economy will **reward self-reliance, innovation, and barter** over traditional business models.

Turning a Crisis Into Long-Term Prosperity

Economic disasters **reset the financial playing field**. Those who prepare **early** will have the chance to **create generational wealth**.

1. Buy Low, Sell High

◈ Land, gold, and essential goods **are cheapest before a collapse.**
◈ **During a crisis, their value skyrockets.**

◈ **Survival Tip:** Buy **valuable assets while others are still focused on cash**—then trade them later for **massive returns**.

2. Develop a Long-Term Wealth Plan

◈ Shift from **traditional money-based wealth** to **real asset wealth**.
◈ Establish **multiple income streams** through investments, skills, and trade.

◈ **Survival Tip:** Wealth isn't just money—it's **access to food, energy, security, and barter networks**.

3. Stay Ahead of the Next Collapse

◈ Financial disasters are **cyclical**—they always happen again.
◈ Once you thrive in **one collapse**, you'll know how to **profit from future ones**.

◈ **Survival Tip: Learning survival economics now** means **you never fear financial crashes again**.

Finalizing Your Post-Collapse Investment Plan

Final Checklist for Alternative Investment Security:

◈ **Gold & Silver** – Inflation-proof wealth storage.
◈ **Land & Farmland** – Essential for food, shelter, and power.
◈ **Essential Goods for Barter** – The new "currency" in a crisis.
◈ **Cryptocurrency** – Money outside the banking system.
◈ **Self-Sufficiency Tools** – Invest in survival and production skills.
◈ **Post-Collapse Business Plan** – Rebuild wealth by **providing what people need**.

◈ **Survival Truth: True wealth isn't paper money—it's control over resources that people can't live without.**

Final Thoughts: Preparing for the Future of Wealth

The next financial collapse will **erase weak investments** and **reward those who planned ahead**. By **investing in alternative assets, securing resources, and adapting to post-collapse economies**, you will **not only survive but thrive** in the new financial landscape.

Chapter 9: Creating a Barter Economy for Local Stability

When financial systems collapse, **cash loses its value, banks freeze withdrawals, and supply chains break down**. In these situations, a **barter economy** naturally emerges, allowing people to trade goods and services **without relying on money**.

A **strong barter network** provides:

◈ Stability in uncertain times
◈ Access to essential goods and services
◈ A functional economy when traditional markets fail

This chapter will teach you **how to build a crisis-proof survival community** by uniting **skills, resources, and trade** to ensure long-term security and success.

Why a Barter Economy Becomes Necessary in a Collapse

In any **economic disaster**, whether it's hyperinflation, financial collapse, or supply chain failure, currency can quickly become **worthless**.

When Money Stops Working

◈ **Hyperinflation** – Money loses purchasing power daily.
◈ **Bank Runs & Freezes** – Withdrawals are limited or blocked.
◈ **Credit & Digital Payments Fail** – Internet outages or government restrictions can cut off access.
◈ **Retail Supply Chains Collapse** – Essential goods disappear from store shelves.

◈ **A barter economy allows people to continue trading, even without cash.**

◈ **Survival Truth:** The **new economy after a collapse** will be based on **necessity, scarcity, and self-reliance.**

Step 1: Identifying the Most Valuable Barter Items

The Best Items to Stockpile for Barter

In a crisis, people don't trade for luxury items—they trade for **necessities**.

◈ **Food & Water** – Canned goods, rice, beans, salt, sugar, honey.
◈ **Medical Supplies** – Painkillers, antibiotics, first aid kits, antiseptics.
◈ **Hygiene Products** – Soap, toothpaste, toilet paper, feminine hygiene.
◈ **Fuel & Energy Sources** – Gasoline, propane, firewood, solar chargers.
◈ **Weapons & Ammunition** – High-value barter items in unstable regions.
◈ **Alcohol & Tobacco** – Always in demand for trade.
◈ **Batteries & Power Banks** – For radios, flashlights, and electronics.
◈ **Seeds & Farming Supplies** – Essential for long-term survival.
◈ **Tools & Repair Equipment** – Hammers, nails, sewing kits, knives.
◈ **Clothing & Footwear** – Durable work boots, jackets, gloves.

◈ **Survival Tip:** The best barter items are **small, lightweight, and have long shelf lives**.

Step 2: Developing Skills for a Trade-Based Economy

If you don't have **physical goods** to barter, your **skills** become your currency.

High-Value Skills for a Barter Economy

⟐ **Medical & First Aid** – Treating wounds, herbal medicine, physical therapy.

⟐ **Food Production** – Gardening, farming, animal husbandry, canning.

⟐ **Construction & Repair** – Carpentry, welding, home security upgrades.

⟐ **Weapons Maintenance & Self-Defense Training** – Gunsmithing, hand-to-hand combat, tactical defense.

⟐ **Alternative Energy Expertise** – Solar panel installation, battery maintenance.

⟐ **Sewing & Textiles** – Mending clothes, making protective gear.

⟐ **Water Purification** – Filtering, distillation, rainwater collection.

⟐ **Survival Tip:** The more **self-reliant skills** you develop, the **more valuable you become in a barter economy**.

Step 3: Building a Crisis-Proof Survival Community

A **lone survivor will struggle**, but a **network of prepared individuals** can create a stable **post-collapse economy**.

How to Form a Barter & Survival Network

◈ **Start Small** – Connect with trusted friends, family, and neighbors.

◈ **Organize Skill-Sharing Meetups** – Exchange knowledge and services.

◈ **Stockpile Trade Goods in a Secure Location** – Have a community storage system.

◈ **Establish Clear Barter Rules** – Avoid conflicts by setting **fair trade values**.

◈ **Create a "Local Currency" System** – Trade using **precious metals, labor hours, or barter credits**.

◈ **Prepare a Safe Meeting Area for Exchanges** – A neutral, secure location to conduct trade.

◈ **Survival Tip:** A **well-organized barter network** strengthens **community security and economic stability**.

Step 4: Protecting Your Trade Economy from Threats

Even in a barter economy, **security risks exist**—theft, looting, and deception.

How to Secure Your Barter Network

◈ **Keep Trading Locations Private** – Avoid publicizing where resources are stored.

◈ **Establish Community Defense Teams** – Train members in **security and perimeter protection.**

◈ **Verify Who You Trade With** – Only barter with **trusted individuals or vetted contacts.**

◈ **Use Discreet Signaling for Trades** – Develop a **low-key trade communication system** (coded messages, word-of-mouth).

◈ **Limit Information Sharing** – Don't tell outsiders what you have.

◈ **Survival Tip:** A barter economy is only as safe as the **security of its members**—always have a **protection plan**.

Step 5: Turning Bartering into a Long-Term Prosperity Model

After the initial **chaos of a collapse**, communities begin to **rebuild**. Those with strong **barter networks and sustainable resources** will thrive in the **new economy**.

How to Build Wealth in a Barter-Based Economy

⟐ **Become a Supplier** – Stockpile **high-demand items** before they become scarce.

⟐ **Specialize in a Valuable Skill** – Offer services that remain in **constant demand.**

⟐ **Control a Resource People Need** – Food, water, energy, and security **become new forms of wealth.**

⟐ **Expand Your Trade Network** – More trading partners mean **greater access to goods.**

⟐ **Invest in Rebuilding & Infrastructure** – As barter evolves, **trade hubs and local markets emerge.**

⟐ **Survival Truth:** In a **post-collapse economy, those who control resources and trade networks become the new wealthy.**

Finalizing Your Barter & Survival Plan

Final Checklist for Building a Barter Economy & Crisis-Proof Community

⟐ **Stockpile High-Demand Barter Items** – Food, medicine, tools, fuel.

⟐ **Learn a Valuable Skill for Trade** – Medical, repair work, farming, security.

⟐ **Form a Local Trade Network** – Build relationships **before** a crisis hits.

⟐ **Establish Secure Trade Rules** – Prevent theft and deception.

⟐ **Prepare for Post-Collapse Rebuilding** – Set up **markets, trade hubs, and labor exchanges.**

⟐ **Survival Truth:** The **first communities to organize a trade system will dominate the post-collapse economy.**

Final Thoughts: The Power of Local Trade in Crisis

A barter economy is more than just survival—it's about **creating stability, rebuilding trust, and ensuring long-term prosperity**.

By developing **a crisis-proof survival community**, securing valuable resources, and building **a network of trade and skills**, you can turn **economic disaster into long-term success**.

Chapter 10: Bouncing Back Stronger After an Economic Collapse

An economic collapse is not the **end of civilization**—it is a **reset**, a chance to rebuild stronger, smarter, and more self-sufficient societies. While the **first phase of collapse** is marked by panic, chaos, and survival struggles, the **next phase** is about **rebuilding stability, prosperity, and governance**.

This final chapter will cover:

◈ **How to rebuild personal and community wealth after an economic collapse**

◈ **How to create a new financial system that thrives without centralized banking**

◈ **How to establish governance and security for long-term stability**

◈ **How to ensure sustainability in food, energy, and commerce for a prosperous future**

By learning from past economic disasters and applying **resilient rebuilding strategies**, we can create **a more stable, self-reliant society** that doesn't repeat the mistakes of the old system.

Step 1: Rebuilding Personal Wealth & Economic Stability

After a financial collapse, wealth isn't measured in **bank accounts or stock portfolios**—it's defined by **assets, resources, and valuable skills.**

How to Restore Personal Financial Security

◈ **Invest in Productive Land** – Land that can produce food, resources, or rental income.

◈ **Restart Small-Scale Trade & Business** – Focus on essential goods and services.

◈ **Use Hard Assets as Wealth Storage** – Gold, silver, food, and energy sources.

◈ **Continue Bartering & Skill-Based Income** – Trade will remain a key part of rebuilding.

◈ **Survival Tip:** The **new financial elite** will be those who **control production and trade**, not those with old, devalued money.

Step 2: Creating a New Financial System

When centralized banking systems collapse, they take down **traditional forms of money, credit, and investment**. The key to **rebuilding a functioning economy** is establishing **alternative financial structures** that work for a decentralized world.

Key Features of a Post-Collapse Financial System

◈ **Commodity-Backed Currency** – Money backed by real assets (gold, silver, food).

◈ **Localized Trade Networks** – Regional economies that **don't rely on global banks**.

◈ **Blockchain & Digital Transactions** – Cryptocurrency or **community-issued credit systems**.

◈ **Mutual Credit & Labor-Based Systems** – Exchange work and services instead of fiat money.

◈ **Survival Tip:** A **community-based economy** backed by real goods and labor **will be more resilient** than any centralized banking system.

Step 3: Establishing Governance & Security in a Post-Collapse Society

One of the greatest risks after an economic collapse is **lawlessness and power struggles**. Without governance, criminal groups and rogue factions **seize control**, leading to prolonged instability.

How to Secure Governance & Leadership in a Rebuilt Society

◈ **Form Local Councils** – Small-scale **governing bodies** to manage trade, security, and resources.

◈ **Create Community Defense Units** – Trained teams to enforce local security and prevent lawlessness.

◈ **Develop Fair Conflict Resolution Systems** – Prevent **vigilante justice** and unfair power grabs.

◈ **Ensure Transparency & Fairness in Leadership** – Leaders must **serve the people, not exploit them.**

◈ **Survival Tip:** The **most successful post-collapse societies** will be those with **stable, well-organized governance structures**.

Step 4: Ensuring Long-Term Sustainability

True economic recovery isn't just about **short-term survival**—it's about creating a **long-term, self-sustaining system** that **thrives without dependence on global markets.**

1. Rebuilding Agriculture & Food Supply Chains

◈ **Community-Run Farms & Permaculture Projects** – Locally owned food production ensures stability.

◈ **Seed Banks & Genetic Diversity** – Avoid dependence on corporate-controlled food systems.

◈ **Food Co-Ops & Local Markets** – Encourage trade within communities instead of large-scale supply chains.

◈ **Survival Tip: Control over food production is control over the economy**—build **independent, self-sufficient food systems.**

2. Developing Energy Independence

◈ **Decentralized Power Grids** – Community-run **solar, wind, and hydro** energy sources.

◈ **Energy Barter Systems** – Trade excess electricity, fuel, or battery storage.

◈ **Alternative Fuel Production** – Biofuels, methane gas, and other off-grid energy sources.

◈ **Survival Tip:** The **post-collapse world will reward those who generate their own power**—build energy independence.

3. Creating a Thriving Trade & Production Economy

◈ **Local Manufacturing & Craftsmanship** – Restart production of essential goods.

◈ **Skill-Based Training Centers** – Teach trades like carpentry, blacksmithing, and textiles.

◈ **Renewable & Sustainable Building Methods** – Avoid wasteful, resource-heavy construction.

◈ **Survival Tip:** Societies that **produce, trade, and innovate** will **rise fastest from economic collapse.**

Step 5: The Path to a New Future

Every financial collapse is an **opportunity to rebuild stronger**—not just to **restore what was lost**, but to create **a better, more resilient system**.

Lessons from History: How Societies Recovered from Collapse

◈ **The Great Depression (1930s)** – Small businesses and local economies thrived while big banks failed.

◈ **Post-WWII Europe** – The rebuilding economy focused on **self-sufficiency and community resilience**.

◈ **Argentina's 2001 Economic Crisis** – Barter networks and local trade saved millions from starvation.

◈ **Survival Truth:** Those who **adapt, organize, and rebuild smarter** will **shape the new economic future**.

Final Checklist for Rebuilding a Thriving Society

◈ **Secure Resources & Sustainable Wealth** – Land, food, energy, and essential commodities.

◈ **Rebuild a Functional Financial System** – Commodity-backed trade, cryptocurrency, and barter.

◈ **Establish Governance & Community Defense** – Protect against lawlessness and power struggles.

◈ **Develop Sustainable Infrastructure** – Agriculture, renewable energy, and skilled labor.

◈ **Encourage Innovation & Adaptation** – Societies that **produce and trade essentials will lead the future**.

◈ **Final Thought:** Economic collapses **reset the system**—but they also offer the **greatest opportunities for those who prepare.**

Final Words: The Strongest Will Rise Again

A financial collapse is not **the end of the world**—it is **a shift in power**. Those who **prepare, adapt, and take action** will **not only survive but build a better future**.

⟐ While **others struggle**, you will **thrive**.

⟐ While **others panic**, you will **lead**.

⟐ While **others collapse**, you will **rise.**

Your knowledge, skills, and preparation will define **the new era of prosperity**—and it starts **now**.

This is your time to take action. Will you be a victim—or a leader of the new world?

Appendix A: Resources for Economic Survival and Investment Strategies

Economic survival requires more than just knowledge—it demands **practical tools, reliable information, and strategic planning**. This appendix provides a **comprehensive list of resources** to help you navigate **financial instability, investment opportunities, and post-collapse economic recovery**.

In this section, you will find:

🔍 **Essential books, websites, and tools for financial preparedness**
🔍 **Alternative investment strategies for wealth protection**
🔍 **Practical survival resources for food, energy, and self-sufficiency**
🔍 **Advanced economic insights for long-term financial growth**

By leveraging these **resources and strategies**, you can **protect your assets, generate income, and ensure long-term prosperity—even in economic turmoil.**

1. Essential Books on Economic Survival & Financial Collapse

Knowledge is power. These books provide **proven strategies** to help you prepare for, survive, and recover from economic crises.

Survival Finance & Economic Preparedness

🔍 *The Death of Money: The Coming Collapse of the International Monetary System* – James Rickards
🔍 *When Money Dies: The Nightmare of the Weimar Hyperinflation* – Adam Fergusson
🔍 *The Creature from Jekyll Island: A Second Look at the Federal Reserve* – G. Edward Griffin
🔍 *Surviving the Economic Collapse* – Fernando "Ferfal" Aguirre
🔍 *The End of Alchemy: Money, Banking, and the Future of the Global Economy* – Mervyn King

Barter & Alternative Trade Systems

◈ *The Art of Barter: How to Trade for Almost Anything* – Karen Hoffman & Shera Dalin

◈ *Barter and Trade for Survival* – Ragnar Benson

◈ *The Barter Economy Handbook* – John Mayer

Investing in Hard Assets & Alternative Wealth Strategies

◈ *Guide to Investing in Gold & Silver: Protect Your Financial Future* – Michael Maloney

◈ *The New Case for Gold* – James Rickards

◈ *Crisis Investing for the Rest of the Decade* – Doug Casey

◈ **Survival Tip:** Always have **physical copies** of essential books—digital files may not be accessible in a crisis.

2. Websites & Online Resources for Financial & Economic Monitoring

These websites provide **real-time updates on financial markets, inflation trends, and alternative investment opportunities.**

Global Economic News & Crisis Monitoring

◈ **ShadowStats** (www.shadowstats.com) – Reports real inflation and unemployment rates.

◈ **Zero Hedge** (www.zerohedge.com) – Alternative financial news and market trends.

◈ **The Daily Reckoning** (www.dailyreckoning.com) – Financial crisis insights and investing advice.

◈ **The Economic Collapse Blog** (www.theeconomiccollapse-blog.com) – Covers financial system weaknesses.

Precious Metals & Hard Asset Investing

◈ **GoldSilver.com** (www.goldsilver.com) – Gold and silver investment education.

◈ **Kitco** (www.kitco.com) – Live market prices for gold, silver, and other metals.

◈ **BullionVault** (www.bullionvault.com) – Secure online gold and silver storage.

Cryptocurrency & Decentralized Finance

◈ **CoinMarketCap** (www.coinmarketcap.com) – Real-time crypto prices and trends.

◈ **Bitcoin.org** (www.bitcoin.org) – The original Bitcoin resource for beginners.

◈ **Monero Outreach** (www.getmonero.org) – Privacy-focused cryptocurrency for secure transactions.

◈ **Survival Tip:** Bookmark these websites and check them **daily** to stay ahead of financial trends.

3. Alternative Investment Strategies for Wealth Protection

1. Gold, Silver & Hard Commodities

◈ **Why Invest?** Gold and silver protect wealth against inflation and financial collapse.

◈ **Where to Buy?** Reputable dealers like **GoldSilver.com, Kitco, and BullionVault**.

◈ **How to Store?** Use a **home safe, private vault, or offshore storage facility**.

◈ **Survival Tip: Silver is better for everyday transactions** while **gold is ideal for storing large amounts of wealth.**

2. Land, Farmland & Real Estate

◈ **Why Invest?** Land is **a finite resource** that provides **food security, housing, and income.**

◈ **Best Investments:**

- **Farmland with water access**
- **Rental properties in stable areas**
- **Homesteads with self-sufficient capabilities**

◈ **Survival Tip:** Rural properties with **food-growing potential** will be **high-value assets in a collapse.**

3. Cryptocurrency & Blockchain Investments

◈ **Why Invest?** Cryptocurrencies provide **financial independence from banks and governments.**

◈ **Best Cryptos for Economic Survival:**

- **Bitcoin (BTC)** – Digital gold for wealth preservation.
- **Monero (XMR)** – Private, untraceable transactions.
- **USDC & DAI** – Stablecoins for currency hedging.

◈ **Survival Tip:** Store crypto in **cold wallets (Ledger, Trezor)** to protect against cyberattacks.

4. Practical Survival Resources for Self-Sufficiency

Food Security & Preservation

◈ **Seed Banks: True Leaf Market, Heirloom Organics, Baker Creek Seeds.**

◈ **Food Storage Supplies: Augason Farms, ReadyWise, Mountain House.**

◈ **DIY Food Preservation Guides:**

- **Canning & Preserving** – USDA Complete Guide to Home Canning.
- **Dehydration & Freeze Drying** – Books by Tammy Gangloff.

◈ **Survival Tip:** Stockpile **at least 12 months' worth** of food to withstand long-term instability.

Energy Independence & Off-Grid Power

◈ **Solar Power Kits: Goal Zero, Renogy, Bluetti.**

◈ **Emergency Generators: Honda, Jackery, EcoFlow Delta.**

◈ **Water Filtration: Berkey, Sawyer, LifeStraw.**

◈ **Survival Tip:** Set up **backup power systems now**—energy shortages happen quickly in economic crises.

5. Advanced Economic Insights for Long-Term Growth

Best Economic & Survival Podcasts

◈ *The Survival Podcast* – Practical self-reliance strategies.

◈ *Wealthion* – Investment and financial crisis strategies.

◈ *Bitcoin Audible* – Crypto and decentralized finance insights.

Best YouTube Channels on Financial Survival

◈ *Chris Martenson – Peak Prosperity* – Economic trends & preparedness.

◈ *Mike Maloney – Hidden Secrets of Money* – Gold, silver, and sound money.

◈ *George Gammon – Rebel Capitalist* – Macro-financial strategies.

◈ **Survival Tip:** Stay **constantly educated**—economic survival requires **lifelong learning**.

Final Thoughts: Your Wealth & Survival Plan Starts Now

A **financial collapse doesn't have to mean financial ruin**—it can be an **opportunity to build lasting wealth and independence.**

Action Plan for Economic Survival & Investment Security

◈ **Diversify Your Wealth** – Gold, silver, land, cryptocurrency, and barter goods.

◈ **Build Alternative Income Streams** – Start businesses, invest in self-sufficiency.

◈ **Prepare for Supply Chain Disruptions** – Stockpile food, energy, and essential trade items.

◈ **Join or Create a Local Barter Network** – Strengthen community resilience.

◈ **Stay Informed & Continuously Learn** – Follow financial trends and adapt to change.

◈ **Final Thought: You have two choices: prepare now or be a victim later. The decision is yours.**

By leveraging these **resources, strategies, and action plans**, you will **not only survive economic collapse**—you will **thrive in the new financial world that follows.**

Message from the Author:

I hope you enjoyed this book, I love astrology and knew there was not a book such as this out on the shelf. I love metaphysical items as well. Please check out my other books:

-Life of Government Benefits

-My life of Hell

-My life with Hydrocephalus

-Red Sky

-World Domination:Woman's rule

-World Domination:Woman's Rule 2: The War

-Life and Banishment of Apophis: book 1

-The Kidney Friendly Diet

-The Ultimate Hemp Cookbook

-Creating a Dispensary(legally)

-Cleanliness throughout life: the importance of showering from childhood to adulthood.

-Strong Roots: The Risks of Overcoddling children

-Hemp Horoscopes: Cosmic Insights and Earthly Healing

- Celestial Hemp Navigating the Zodiac: Through the Green Cosmos

-Astrological Hemp: Aligning The Stars with Earth's Ancient Herb

-The Astrological Guide to Hemp: Stars, Signs, and Sacred Leaves

-Green Growth: Innovative Marketing Strategies for your Hemp Products and Dispensary

-Cosmic Cannabis

-Astrological Munchies

-Henry The Hemp

-Zodiacal Roots: The Astrological Soul Of Hemp

- Green Constellations: Intersection of Hemp and Zodiac

-Hemp in The Houses: An astrological Adventure Through The Cannabis Galaxy

-Galactic Ganja Guide

Heavenly Hemp

Zodiac Leaves

Doctor Who Astrology

Cannastrology

Stellar Satvias and Cosmic Indicas

Celestial Cannabis: A Zodiac Journey

AstroHerbology: The Sky and The Soil: Volume 1

AstroHerbology:Celestial Cannabis:Volume 2

Cosmic Cannabis Cultivation

The Starry Guide to Herbal Harmony: Volume 1

The Starry Guide to Herbal Harmony: Cannabis Universe: Volume 2

Yugioh Astrology: Astrological Guide to Deck, Duels and more

Nightmare Mansion: Echoes of The Abyss

Nightmare Mansion 2: Legacy of Shadows

Nightmare Mansion 3: Shadows of the Forgotten

Nightmare Mansion 4: Echoes of the Damned

The Life and Banishment of Apophis: Book 2

Nightmare Mansion: Halls of Despair

Healing with Herb: Cannabis and Hydrocephalus

Planetary Pot: Aligning with Astrological Herbs: Volume 1

Fast Track to Freedom: 30 Days to Financial Independence Using AI, Assets, and Agile Hustles

Cosmic Hemp Pathways

How to Become Financially Free in 30 Days: 10,000 Paths to Prosperity

Zodiacal Herbage: Astrological Insights: Volume 1

Nightmare Mansion: Whispers in the Walls

The Daleks Invade Atlantis

Henry the hemp and Hydrocephalus

10X The Kidney Friendly Diet

Cannabis Universe: Adult coloring book

Hemp Astrology: The Healing Power of the Stars

Zodiacal Herbage: Astrological Insights: Cannabis Universe: Volume 2

Planetary Pot: Aligning with Astrological Herbs: Cannabis Universes: Volume 2

Doctor Who Meets the Replicators and SG-1: The Ultimate Battle for Survival

Nightmare Mansion: Curse of the Blood Moon

The Celestial Stoner: A Guide to the Zodiac

Cosmic Pleasures: Sex Toy Astrology for Every Sign

Hydrocephalus Astrology: Navigating the Stars and Healing Waters

Lapis and the Mischievous Chocolate Bar

Celestial Positions: Sexual Astrology for Every Sign

Apophis's Shadow Work Journal: **:** A Journey of Self-Discovery and Healing

Kinky Cosmos: Sexual Kink Astrology for Every Sign

Digital Cosmos: The Astrological Digimon Compendium

Stellar Seeds: The Cosmic Guide to Growing with Astrology

Apophis's Daily Gratitude Journal

Cat Astrology: Feline Mysteries of the Cosmos

The Cosmic Kama Sutra: An Astrological Guide to Sexual Positions

Unleash Your Potential: A Guided Journal Powered by AI Insights

Whispers of the Enchanted Grove

Cosmic Pleasures: An Astrological Guide to Sexual Kinks

369, 12 Manifestation Journal

Whisper of the nocturne journal(blank journal for writing or drawing)

The Boogey Book

Locked In Reflection: A Chastity Journey Through Locktober

Generating Wealth Quickly:How to Generate $100,000 in 24 Hours

Star Magic: Harness the Power of the Universe

The Flatulence Chronicles: A Fart Journal for Self-Discovery

The Doctor and The Death Moth

Seize the Day: A Personal Seizure Tracking Journal

The Ultimate Boogeyman Safari: A Journey into the Boogie World and Beyond

Whispers of Samhain: 1,000 Spells of Love, Luck, and Lunar Magic: Samhain Spell Book

Apophis's guides:Witch's Spellbook Crafting Guide for Halloween

Frost & Flame: The Enchanted Yule Grimoire of 1000 Winter Spells

The Ultimate Boogey Goo Guide & Spooky Activities for Halloween Fun

Harmony of the Scales: A Libra's Spellcraft for Balance and Beauty

The Enchanted Advent: 36 Days of Christmas Wonders

Nightmare Mansion: The Labyrinth of Screams

Harvest of Enchantment: 1,000 Spells of Gratitude, Love, and Fortune for Thanksgiving

The Boogey Chronicles: A Journal of Nightly Encounters and Shadowy Secrets

The 12 Days of Financial Freedom: A Step-by-Step Christmas Countdown to Transform Your Finances

Sigil of the Eternal Spiral Blank Journal

A Christmas Feast: Timeless Recipes for Every Meal

Holiday Stress-Free Solutions: A Survival Guide to Thriving During the Festive Season

Yu-Gi-Oh! Holiday Gifting Mastery: The Ultimate Guide for Fans and Newcomers Alike

Holiday Harmony: A Hydrocephalus Survival Guide for the Festive Season

Celestial Craft: The Witch's Almanac for 2025 – A Cosmic Guide to Manifestations, Moons, and Mystical Events

Doctor Who: The Toymaker's Winter Wonderland

Tulsa King Unveiled: A Thrilling Guide to Stallone's Mafia Masterpiece

Pendulum Craft: A Complete Guide to Crafting and Using Personalized Divination Tools

Nightmare Mansion: Santa's Eternal Eve

Starlight Noel: A Cosmic Journey through Christmas Mysteries

The Dark Architect: Unlocking the Blueprint of Existence

Surviving the Embrace: The Ultimate Guide to Encounters with The Hugging Molly

The Enchanted Codex: Secrets of the Craft for Witches, Wiccans, and Pagans

Harvest of Gratitude: A Complete Thanksgiving Guide

Yuletide Essentials: A Complete Guide to an Authentic and Magical Christmas

Celestial Smokes: A Cosmic Guide to Cigars and Astrology

Living in Balance: A Comprehensive Survival Guide to Thriving with Diabetes Insipidus

Cosmic Symbiosis: The Venom Zodiac Chronicles

The Cursed Paw of Ambition

Cosmic Symbiosis: The Astrological Venom Journal

Celestial Wonders Unfold: A Stargazer's Guide to the Cosmos (2024-2029)

The Ultimate Black Friday Prepper's Guide: Mastering Shopping Strategies and Savings

Cosmic Sales: The Astrological Guide to Black Friday Shopping

Legends of the Corn Mother and Other Harvest Myths

Whispers of the Harvest: The Corn Mother's Journal

The Evergreen Spellbook

The Doctor Meets the Boogeyman

The White Witch of Rose Hall's SpellBook

The Gingerbread Golem's Shadow: A Study in Sweet Darkness

The Gingerbread Golem Codex: An Academic Exploration of Sweet Myths

The Gingerbread Golem Grimoire: Sweet Magicks and Spells for the Festive Witch

The Curse of the Gingerbread Golem

10-minute Christmas Crafts for kids

Christmas Crisis Solutions: The Ultimate Last-Minute Survival Guide

Gingerbread Golem Recipes: Holiday Treats with a Magical Twist

The Infinite Key: Unlocking Mystical Secrets of the Ages

Enchanted Yule: A Wiccan and Pagan Guide to a Magical and Memorable Season

Dinosaurs of Power: Unlocking Ancient Magick

Astro-Dinos: The Cosmic Guide to Prehistoric Wisdom

Gallifrey's Yule Logs: A Festive Doctor Who Cookbook

The Dino Grimoire: Secrets of Prehistoric Magick

The Gift They Never Knew They Needed

The Gingerbread Golem's Culinary Alchemy: Enchanting Recipes for a Sweetly Dark Feast

A Time Lord Christmas: Holiday Adventures with the Doctor

Krampusproofing Your Home: Defensive Strategies for Yule

Silent Frights: A Collection of Christmas Creepypastas to Chill Your Bones

Santa Raptor's Jolly Carnage: A Dino-Claus Christmas Tale

Prehistoric Palettes: A Dino Wicca Coloring Journey

The Christmas Wishkeeper Chronicles

The Starlight Sleigh: A Holiday Journey

Elf Secrets: The True Magic of the North Pole

Candy Cane Conjurations

Cooking with Kids: Recipes Under 20 Minutes

Doctor Who: The TARDIS Confiscation

The Anxiety First Aid Kit: Quick Tools to Calm Your Mind

Frosty Whispers: A Winter's Tale

The Infinite Key: Unlocking the Secrets to Prosperity, Resilience, and Purpose

The Grasping Void: Why You'll Regret This Purchase

Astrology for Busy Bees: Star Signs Simplified

The Instant Focus Formula: Cut Through the Noise

The Secret Language of Colors: Unlocking the Emotional Codes

Sacred Fossil Chronicles: Blank Journal

The Christmas Cottage Miracle

Feeding Frenzy: Graboid-Inspired Recipes

Manifest in Minutes: The Quick Law of Attraction Guide

The Symbiote Chronicles: Doctor Who's Venomous Journey

Think Tiny, Grow Big: The Minimalist Mindset

The Energy Key: Unlocking Limitless Motivation

New Year, New Magic: Manifesting Your Best Year Yet

Unstoppable You: Mastering Confidence in Minutes

Infinite Energy: The Secret to Never Feeling Drained

Lightning Focus: Mastering the Art of Productivity in a Distracted World

Saturnalia Manifestation Magick: A Guide to Unlocking Abundance During the Solstice

Graboids and Garland: The Ultimate Tremors-Themed Christmas Guide

12 Nights of Holiday Magic

The Power of Pause: 60-Second Mindfulness Practices

The Quick Reset: How to Reclaim Your Life After Burnout
The Shadow Eater: A Tale of Despair and Survival
The Micro-Mastery Method: Transform Your Skills in Just Minutes a Day
Reclaiming Time: How to Live More by Doing Less
Chronovore: The Eternal Nexus
The Mind Reset: Unlocking Your Inner Peace in a Chaotic World
Confidence Code: Building Unshakable Self-Belief
Baby the Vampire Terrier
Baby the Vampire Terrier's Christmas Adventure
Celestial Streams: The Content Creator's Astrology Manual
The Wealth Whisperer: Unlocking Abundance with Everyday Actions
The Energy Equation: Maximize Your Output Without Burning Out
The Happiness Algorithm: Science-Backed Steps to Joyful Living
Stress-Free Success: Achieving Goals Without Anxiety
Mindful Wealth: The New Blueprint for Financial Freedom
The Festive Flavors of New Year: A Culinary Celebration
The Master's Gambit: Keys of Eternal Power
Shadowed Secrets: Groundhog Day Mysteries
Beneath the Burrow: Lessons from the Groundhog
Spring's Whispers: The Groundhog's Prediction
The Limitless Mindset: Unlock Your Untapped Potential
The Focus Funnel: How to Cut Through Chaos and Get Results
Bold Moves: Building Courage to Live on Your Terms
The Daily Shift: Simple Practices for Lasting Transformation
The Quarter-Life Reset: Thriving in Your 20s and 30s
The Art of Shadowplay: Building Your Own Personal Myth
The Eternal Loop: Finding Purpose in Repetition
Burrowing Wisdom: Life Lessons from the Groundhog
Shadow Work: A Groundhog Day Perspective
Love in Bloom: 5-Minute Romantic Gestures

The Shadowspell Codex: Secrets of Forbidden Magick
The Burnout Cure: Finding Balance in a Busy World
The Groundhog Prophecy: Unlocking Seasonal Secrets
Nog Tales: The Spirited History of Eggnog
Six More Weeks: Embracing Seasonal Transitions
The Lumivian Chronicles: Fragments of the Fifth Dimension
Money on Your Mind: A Beginner's Guide to Wealth
The Focus Fix: Breaking Through Distraction
January's Spirit Keepers: Mystical Protectors of the Cold
Creativity Unchained: Unlocking Your Wildest Ideas in 2025
Manifestation Mastery: 365 Days to Rewrite Your Reality
The Groundhog's Mirror: Reflecting on Change
The Weeping Angels' Christmas Curse
Burrowed in Time: A Groundhog Day Journey
Heartbeats: Poems to Share with Your Valentine
Dino Wicca: The Sacred Grimoire of Prehistoric Magick
Courage of the Pride: Finding Your Inner Roar
The Lion's Leap: Bold Moves for Big Results
Healthy Hustle: Achieving Without Overworking
Practical Manifesting: Turning Dreams into Reality in 2025
Jurassic Pharaohs: Unlocking the Magick of Ancient Egypt and Dino Wicca
The Happiness Equation: Small Changes for Big Joy
The Confidence Compass: Finding Your Inner Strength
Whispers in the Hollow: Tales of the Forgotten Beasts
Echoes from the Hollow: The Return of Forgotten Beasts
The Hollow Ascendant: The Rise of the Forgotten Beasts
The Relationship Reset: Building Better Connections
Mastering the Morning: How to Win the Day Before 8 AM
The Shadow's Dance: Groundhog Day Symbolism
Cupid's Kitchen: Quick Valentine's Day Recipes
Valentine's Day on a Budget: Love Without Breaking the Bank
Astrocraft: Aligning the Stars in the World of Minecraft

Forecasting Life: Groundhog Day Reflections

Bleeding Hearts: Twisted Tales of Valentine's Terror

Herbal Smoke Revolution: The Ultimate Guide to Nature's Cigarette Alternative

Winter's Wrath: The Complete Survival Blueprint for Extreme Freezes.

The Groundhog's Shadow: A Tale of Seasons

Burrowed Insights: Wisdom from the Groundhog

Sensual Strings: The Art of Erotic Bondage

Whispered Flames: Unlocking the Power of Fire Play

Forgotten Shadows: A Guide to Cryptids Lost to Time

Six Weeks of Secrets: Groundhog Day's Hidden Messages

Shadows and Cycles: Groundhog Day Reflections

The Art of Love Letters: Crafting the Perfect Message

Romantic Getaways at Home: Turning Your Space into Paradise

Purrfect Brews: A Cat Lover's Guide to Coffee and Companionship

The Groundhog's Wisdom: Timeless Lessons for Modern Life

The Shadow Oracle: Groundhog Day as a Predictor

Emerging from the Burrow: A Journey of Renewal

The Language of Love: Learning Your Partner's Love Style

Authorpreneur: The Ultimate Blueprint for Writing, Publishing, and Thriving as an Author

Weathering the Seasons: Groundhog Day Perspectives

Valentine's Day Magic: A Guide to Romantic Rituals

The Shadow Chronicles: Stories of Groundhog Day

Love and Laughter: Fun Games for Valentine's Day

AstroRealty: Unlocking the Stars for Property Success

The Groundhog's Path: A Guide to Seasonal Balance

Groundhog Day Diaries: Reflections in the Shadow

The Groundhog's Light: Illuminating the Path Ahead

Valentine's Traditions from Around the World

AI Wealth Revolution: Unlocking the Trillionaire Mindset
Love Rekindled: Reigniting Passion in Relationships
Single and Thriving: Self-Love on Valentine's Day
Emerald Legends: Mystical Tales of Ireland
Green Alchemy: Harnessing Nature's Magic
The Hearts of Horror: A Valentine's Day Nightmare
The Leprechaun's Guide to Wealth and Wisdom
Dancing with the Sidhe: Celebrating the Otherworld
Shamrocks and Shadows: Mysteries of the Green Isle
Emerald Energy: Harnessing Luck and Growth
The Gingerbread Golem's Valentine: A Sweetheart's Guide to Love and Enchantment
The Celtic Knot: Weaving Life and Destiny
Green Fire: Elemental Magic for St. Patrick's Day
Clover Chronicles: Finding Your Inner Luck
Ireland's Mystical Creatures: A Field Guide
Gingerbread Golem's Love Almanac
Prowl and Thrive: The Lion's Guide to Success
Love Alchemy: Transforming Your Life Through Heart Energy
WORLD DOMINATION: Woman's Rule 3:The New Life
The Midnight Rose: A Guide to Lunar Love Spells
The Forbidden Letters: Writing Your Own Love Prophecy
Luck and Lore: St. Patrick's Day for Modern Mystics
The Green Path: A Pagan Celebration of Renewal
The Dark Architect's Guide to Reprogramming Reality
Prankster's Paradise: A Guide to Harmless Hijinks
Manifest Your Reality: The Law of Attraction Simplified
The TARDIS Owner's Manual: Understanding the Doctor's Ship: *A complete guide to the TARDIS, its technology, secrets, and mysteries*
Starlit Romance: Astrology Secrets for Finding True Love

The Time Lord's Atlas: A Complete Guide to the Whoniverse: *A breakdown of the locations, planets, and dimensions explored in Doctor Who*

Sweetheart Shadows: The Dark Side of Love and Attraction

February Fire: Reigniting Passion in Every Area of Life

The Self-Love Toolkit: 5 Ways to Embrace Who You Are

February Sparks: Ignite Your Dreams in 28 Days

March to Success: A 31-Day Action Blueprint

Ancient Paths: The 13 Sacred Principles of Dino Wicca

Echoes of Tomorrow: Navigating the AI Revolution

The Wellness Blueprint: Balancing Mind, Body, and Soul

Green Horizons: Sustainable Living for a Better Tomorrow

The AI Wealth Code: How to Make Millions with Automation

AI-Powered Creativity: Writing, Art, and Music for Profit

Extinction Rites: Rebirthing Your Soul Through Prehistoric Magick

Sacred Serpents tarot

Celestial Enchantment blank journal

Star Strains

Culinary Journeys: Exploring Global Flavors at Home

The Hollowvale Curse

The Hollowvale Harvest

The Egg of Transformation: Awakening Your Inner Power

Blooming Into Power: A Wiccan Guide to Spring Awakening

The Nightmare Nexus: The Third Doctor's Perilous Haunting

Digital Detox: Reclaiming Your Life in a Connected World

Ostara's Path: Walking the Spiral of Renewal

The Sacred Hare

Financial Freedom: Building Wealth in the Modern Age

Spring's Cauldron: Stirring the Waters of Change

The Hollowvale Pact

Quantum Consciousness: The Science of Reality Shifting

The Hollowvale Hunger

The Sacred Waters Within: A Witch's Guide to Hydrocephalus Magick

The Raven's Nest: Building a Life of Unshakable Stability

AI and the Human Mind: The Future of Intelligence

The Hollowvale Reckoning

Timeless Love: Building and Maintaining Lasting Relationships

The Raven's Roar: Unlocking Unstoppable Confidence

Raven Sight: Awakening Intuition and Inner Wisdom

The Butterfly Effect: Small Changes, Big Transformations

Taming the Boogeyman: How to Conquer Your Inner Fears

The Magick of Green: Awakening Earth's Energy in You

The Entrepreneurial Mindset: Secrets to Business Success

The Hollowvale End

The Shadow Luck Ritual: Reclaiming Power from Your Dark Side

Spring Magick for Beginners: A Simple Guide to Seasonal Energy Work

Doctor Who: The Hollowvale Conundrum

The March of Miracles: Unlocking Synchronicities in Spring

Unveiling the Cosmos: A Guide to Stargazing and Space Exploration

If you want solar for your home go here: https://www.harborsolar.live/apophisenterprises/

Get Some Tarot cards: https://www.makeplayingcards.com/sell/apophis-occult-shop

Get some shirts: https://www.bonfire.com/store/apophis-shirt-emporium/

<u>Instagrams:</u>
@apophis_enterprises,
@apophisbookemporium,
@apophisscardshop
Twitter: @apophisenterpr1
Tiktok:@apophisenterprise
Youtube: @sg1fan23477, @FiresideRetreatKingdom
Hive: @sg1fan23477
CheeLee: @SG1fan23477

Podcast: Apophis Chat Zone: https://open.spotify.com/show/5zXbrCLEV2xzCp8ybrfHsk?si=fb4d4fdbdce44dec

Newsletter: https://apophiss-newsletter-27c897.beehiiv.com/

If you want to support me or see posts of other projects that I have come over to: **buymeacoffee.com/mpetchinskg**

I post there daily several times a day

Get your Dinowicca or Christmas themed digital products, especially Santa Raptor songs and other musics. Here: **https://sg1fan23477.gumroad.com**

Apophis Yuletide Digital has not only digital Christmas items, but it will have all things with Dinowicca as well as other Digital products.

www.ingramcontent.com/pod-product-compliance
Lightning Source LLC
LaVergne TN
LVHW022012200926
848481LV00007B/2352
* 9 7 9 8 3 4 8 5 8 4 5 3 5 *